THE INNER STRENGTH WORKBOOK FOR TEENS

Stop Self-Doubt, Start Self-Love

Practical CBT & DBT Exercises to Build Confidence,
Overcome Comparison, and Believe in Yourself

Richard Bass

3 FREE Bonuses!

- **Positive Discipline Playbook:** Dive into 50 powerful strategies designed to unleash your child's full potential through positive guidance. Say goodbye to tantrums and hello to harmony!

- **Kids' Planner:** Get organized and empower your child with this fun and interactive planner. From homework schedules to goal-setting, watch them blossom with confidence!

- **The Positive Self-Talk Guide:** Help your teen transform negative thoughts into powerful affirmations! This practical toolkit includes daily exercises, reframing techniques, and 50+ positive self-talk starters. Watch them shift from self-doubt to self-confidence!

Stop Self-Doubt, Start Self-Love

Practical CBT & DBT Exercises to Build Confidence,
Overcome Comparison, and Believe in Yourself

CONTENTS

Introduction

"You yourself, as much as anybody in the entire universe, deserve your love and affection."
- Buddha

Research shows that nearly 70% of teenagers struggle with low self-esteem at some point during their adolescent years (American Psychological Association, 2023). If you've picked up this workbook, you might be one of them. Maybe you find yourself constantly comparing yourself to others, feeling like you're not good enough, or struggling to speak up for yourself. Perhaps you spend hours criticizing your appearance, doubting your abilities, or avoiding new experiences because you're afraid of failing.

You're not alone, and more importantly, you're not stuck with these feelings forever.

Self-esteem isn't something you're born with or without—it's a skill that can be developed and strengthened over time. Just like building muscle at the gym, building confidence requires the right exercises, consistent practice, and patience with yourself as you grow.

This workbook combines two powerful therapeutic approaches that have helped millions of people build genuine, lasting confidence: Cognitive Behavioral Therapy (CBT) and Dialectical Behavior Therapy (DBT). Don't let the fancy names intimidate you—these are simply proven methods for changing negative thought patterns, managing difficult emotions, and building healthier relationships with yourself and others.

What Makes This Workbook Different

Unlike other self-help books that just tell you to *"think positive,"* this workbook gives you specific, research-backed tools that actually work. You'll learn how to:

- Identify and challenge the inner critic that keeps you feeling small
- Break free from the comparison trap that social media creates
- Discover your unique strengths and values
- Handle setbacks without letting them destroy your confidence
- Build healthy boundaries in relationships
- Create daily habits that naturally boost your self-worth

How CBT and DBT Help Build Self-Esteem

<u>**Cognitive Behavioral Therapy (CBT)**</u> teaches you that your thoughts, feelings, and behaviors are all connected. When you have negative thoughts about yourself (*"I'm so stupid," "Nobody likes me"*), those thoughts create negative feelings (sadness, anxiety, shame), which then lead to behaviors that actually make you feel worse (avoiding people, giving up easily, not trying new things).

The good news is that this cycle works in reverse too. When you learn to recognize and change negative thought patterns, your feelings and behaviors naturally improve. CBT gives you practical tools to become your own best advocate instead of your harshest critic.

<u>**Dialectical Behavior Therapy (DBT)**</u> focuses on helping you manage intense emotions and build better relationships. It teaches skills like emotional regulation (staying calm when you're upset), distress tolerance (handling difficult situations without making them worse), and interpersonal effectiveness (communicating your needs clearly and setting healthy boundaries).

Together, CBT and DBT create a powerful toolkit for building authentic self-confidence that comes from within, not from external validation.

Who This Workbook Is For

This workbook is designed for teenagers aged 13-19 who want to:

- Feel more confident in social situations
- Stop the constant self-criticism and negative self-talk
- Build resilience to handle life's challenges
- Develop healthy relationships based on mutual respect
- Discover their unique strengths and values
- Create lasting habits that support their mental health

How to Use This Workbook

The best part about this workbook is that you can use it at your own pace, in the privacy of your own space. You don't need a therapist or counselor to benefit from these exercises, though having professional support is always valuable if you're struggling with more serious mental health concerns.

Here's how to get the most out of your experience:

- **Go at Your Own Pace:** There's no rush. Some exercises might feel easy, while others might bring up difficult emotions. Take breaks when you need them, and don't pressure yourself to complete everything quickly.

- **Be Honest:** The exercises only work if you're truthful with yourself. Nobody else has to see your answers unless you choose to share them.

- **Practice Regularly:** Like any skill, building self-esteem requires consistent practice. Try to spend 10-15 minutes a day working through exercises or reflecting on what you've learned.

- **Be Patient and Kind to Yourself:** Change takes time, and there will be setbacks. Treat yourself with the same kindness you'd show a good friend who was struggling.

- **Seek Support When Needed:** If you're dealing with depression, anxiety, trauma, or thoughts of self-harm, please reach out to a trusted adult, counselor, or mental health professional. This workbook is a valuable supplement to professional care, not a replacement for it.

What to Expect

As you work through this book, you might notice:
- Increased awareness of your thought patterns
- Better ability to manage difficult emotions
- More confidence in social situations
- Improved relationships with family and friends
- Greater resilience when facing challenges
- A stronger sense of who you are and what you value

Remember, building self-esteem isn't about becoming perfect or never having doubts again. It's about developing a healthy, realistic relationship with yourself—one based on self-compassion, personal growth, and authentic confidence.

A Note About Difficult Emotions

Some exercises in this workbook might bring up uncomfortable feelings or memories. This is normal and often part of the healing process. However, if you ever feel overwhelmed or unsafe, please stop and reach out for support from a trusted adult or mental health professional.

If you're having thoughts of self-harm or suicide, please contact:
- National Suicide Prevention Lifeline: 988
- Crisis Text Line: Text HOME to 741741
- Or go to your nearest emergency room

Your life has value, and there are people who want to help you through difficult times.

READY TO BEGIN?

READY TO BEGIN?

You've already taken the most important step by deciding to invest in yourself. The journey to genuine self-confidence starts now, and every small step you take matters. Be proud of yourself for choosing growth over staying stuck, and for believing that you deserve to feel good about who you are.

Let's build your confidence together, one exercise at a time.

Chapter 1

Understanding Your Inner Voice

"You have been critical of yourself for years, and it hasn't worked. Try approving of yourself and see what happens."

- Louise Hay

Your inner voice is constantly talking to you throughout the day. Sometimes it's encouraging and supportive, but often it can be harsh and critical. This inner critic developed over time through various experiences, feedback from others, and societal messages. The good news is that just as you learned these critical thought patterns, you can also learn to change them.

CBT teaches us that our thoughts directly impact how we feel about ourselves. When we have negative thoughts like *"I'm not good enough"* or *"Everyone is better than me,"* our self-esteem drops. But when we learn to recognize and challenge these thoughts, we can build genuine confidence from within.

The exercises in this chapter will help you become aware of your inner critic and start replacing harsh self-talk with more balanced, compassionate thoughts.

EXERCISE 1

The Inner Critic Detective

Your inner critic often speaks so automatically that you don't even notice it's happening. This exercise helps you catch those critical thoughts as they occur.

- ### *Instructions:*

For the next three days, carry a small notebook or use your phone to record critical thoughts about yourself. Each time you notice a harsh or negative thought about yourself, write it down immediately. Don't judge the thought or try to change it yet—just notice and record it.

_____

_____

_____

_____

_____

_____

_____

_____

_____

_____

_____

_____

_____

_____

_____

After three days, look at your list and circle the three most common critical thoughts. These are your *"top critics"* that we'll work on changing in the next exercises.

My Top 3 Critical Thoughts:

_____

_____

_____

_____

_____

_____

_____

Thought Record Tracker

This exercise helps you understand the connection between your thoughts, feelings, and situations. When you know what triggers your inner critic, you can be better prepared to respond differently.

- ## Instructions:

Think of recent situations where you felt bad about yourself. Fill out the table below to understand what happened.

Situation (What happened?)	Thought (What went through your mind?)	Feeling (How did you feel?)	Body Sensation (What did you notice in your body?)

Reflection:

- What patterns do you notice? Are certain situations more likely to trigger your inner critic?

_____

_____

_____

_____

_____

_____

_____

EXERCISE 3

Evidence Court

When your inner critic makes harsh judgments about you, it's time to take those thoughts to *"court."* This CBT technique helps you examine whether your critical thoughts are actually true or if they're exaggerated.

- ## *Instructions:*

Choose one critical thought from Exercise 1. Write it at the top of the space below, then gather evidence for and against this thought, as if you were a detective building a case.

My Critical Thought:

_____

_____

_____

_____

Evidence FOR this thought *(Why it might be true)*	Evidence AGAINST this thought *(Why it might not be true)*

The Verdict:

- Based on the evidence, what's a more balanced way to think about this situation?

_____

_____

_____

_____

_____

_____

_____

EXERCISE 4

Rewrite Your Story

Your inner critic often tells you a story about who you are, but that story might not be accurate or complete. This exercise helps you create a more balanced narrative about yourself.

- *Instructions:*

Think about how your inner critic would describe you in a few sentences. Write that version first, then rewrite it from the perspective of a kind, supportive friend who knows you well.

Inner Critic Version:

_____

_____

_____

_____

_____

_____

_____

_____

_____

Supportive Friend Version:

_____

_____

_____

_____

_____

_____

_____

_____

Which version feels more accurate and helpful?

Circle one above.

The Compassionate Friend Technique

When you're struggling with self-criticism, imagine what you would say to your best friend if they were going through the same situation. We're often much kinder to others than we are to ourselves.

- ### *Instructions:*

Think of a current situation where you're being hard on yourself. Write down what your inner critic is saying, then respond as you would to a good friend facing the same challenge.

Situation I'm being hard on myself about:

_____

_____

_____

_____

_____

- ### What my inner critic says:

_____

_____

_____

_____

_____

_____

_____

_____

- What I would tell my best friend in this same situation:

_____

_____

_____

_____

_____

_____

_____

_____

_____

 For the next week, try speaking to yourself with the same kindness you'd show a good friend.

Journal Prompts for Continued Growth

Take time to reflect on these questions in your own journal or notebook:

1.

When did you first notice your inner critic becoming harsh? Was there a specific event or period in your life?

2.

Who in your life speaks to you with kindness and encouragement? How can you internalize their supportive voice?

3.

What would change in your daily life if you were less critical of yourself?

4.

What are three kind things you can say to yourself when you notice the inner critic getting loud?

5.

How do you think your relationships would improve if you treated yourself with more compassion?

Chapter

Breaking Free from Comparison Traps

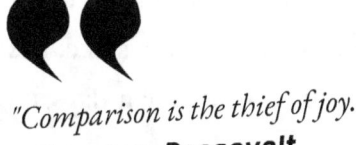

"Comparison is the thief of joy."
- Theodore Roosevelt

In today's world, it's almost impossible to avoid comparing yourself to others. Social media feeds are filled with highlight reels, classmates seem to have it all figured out, and everywhere you look, someone appears to be doing better than you. But here's the truth: comparison rarely shows you the full picture, and it's one of the fastest ways to destroy your self-confidence.

CBT teaches us that comparison-based thinking often involves cognitive distortions—twisted ways of thinking that make situations seem worse than they actually are. When we compare ourselves to others, we tend to compare our behind-the-scenes struggles with everyone else's highlight reel, which creates an unfair and unrealistic standard.

The exercises in this chapter will help you recognize when you're falling into comparison traps and give you tools to refocus on your own unique journey and progress.

EXERCISE 6

Social Media Reality Check

Social media often shows everyone's highlight reel, not their real life. This exercise helps you see the difference between online personas and reality.

- ### Instructions:

Pick 3 people you follow who seem to have *"perfect"* lives. For each person, write down what their posts make you think their life is like, then imagine what their real day might include (homework stress, family arguments, bad hair days, etc.).

- ### Person 1:
  - What their posts suggest:

  _____

  _____

  _____

  - What their real life probably includes:

  _____

  _____

  _____

- *Person 2:*
  - What their posts suggest:

  _____

  _____

  _____

  - What their real life probably includes:

  _____

  _____

  _____

- *Person 3:*
  - What their posts suggest:

  _____

  _____

  _____

  - What their real life probably includes:

  _____

  _____

  _____

Reflection:

- How does this change how their posts make you feel about yourself?

_____

_____

_____

_____

_____

My Unique Qualities Inventory

Instead of focusing on what others have that you don't, this exercise helps you identify what makes you uniquely valuable.

- ## *Instructions:*

Fill out each category below. If you get stuck, ask a trusted friend or family member to help you see your positive qualities.

Category	My Unique Qualities
Personality traits that make me a good friend	
Skills or talents I'm naturally good at	
Ways I've helped others recently	
Challenges I've overcome	
Things I'm curious about or passionate about	
Compliments I receive regularly	
Ways I make people laugh or feel good	
Values that are important to me	

- Which quality from above are you most proud of and why?

_____

_____

_____

_____

_____

_____

EXERCISE 8

The Comparison Journal

This exercise helps you catch yourself in the act of comparing and practice redirecting your thoughts.

- *Instructions:*

For one week, each time you notice yourself comparing yourself to someone else, write it down and then reframe it.

When did this happen?	What comparison did I make?	How can I reframe this more positively?

- What patterns do you notice in your comparison habits?

_____

_____

_____

_____

_____

Spotlight Effect Challenge

The spotlight effect is when we think everyone is paying attention to our flaws, but in reality, most people are too busy thinking about themselves to notice our imperfections.

- **Instructions:**

Think of a recent situation where you felt embarrassed or self-conscious. Answer the questions below to get perspective on whether it was really as noticeable as you thought.

Situation that made me feel self-conscious:

_____

_____

_____

_____

How much attention do I think people paid to this? (1-10 scale)

- *Circle one:*   1   2   3   4   5   6   7   8   9   10

How much attention do people probably actually paid to this? (1-10 scale)

- *Circle one:*   1   2   3   4   5   6   7   8   9   10

Three things other people were probably thinking about instead:

_____

_____

_____

_____

_____

_____

How does this perspective change how you feel about the situation?

_____

_____

_____

_____

_____

_____

Create Your Personal Highlight Reel

Instead of only seeing others' highlight reels, create your own to remind yourself of your accomplishments and positive moments.

- ## *Instructions:*

Fill out your personal highlight reel for the past month. Include both big and small wins.

- ## Academic/School Highlights:

_____

_____

_____

_____

- ## Social/Friendship Highlights:

_____

_____

_____

_____

- **Personal Growth Highlights:**

_____

_____

_____

_____

- **Fun/Creative Highlights:**

_____

_____

_____

_____

- **Acts of Kindness (given or received):**

_____

_____

_____

_____

Choose your top 3 highlights from above
and write why each one makes you proud:

1. _____

   _____

   _____

2. _____

   _____

   _____

3. _____

   _____

   _____

Update this highlight reel monthly and look back
at it whenever comparison thoughts creep in.

Journal Prompts for Continued Growth

Take time to reflect on these questions in your own journal or notebook:

1.

What would your life look like if you completely stopped comparing yourself to others?

2.

Who are three people you admire for reasons that have nothing to do with appearance or material possessions?

3.

What accomplishment are you most proud of that might not seem impressive to others but matters deeply to you?

4.

How do you feel when someone compares themselves negatively to you? What would you want to tell them?

5.

What would you tell a younger sibling or friend who was constantly comparing themselves to others?

Chapter 3

Discovering Your Strengths and Values

"When you know your worth, no one can make you feel worthless."
- Unknown

T rue confidence doesn't come from being perfect or having what everyone else has—it comes from knowing who you are, what you're good at, and what matters to you. Many teens struggle with confidence because they haven't taken the time to discover their unique strengths and personal values.

Your strengths are the things you naturally do well, while your values are the principles and beliefs that guide your decisions and give your life meaning. When you operate from your strengths and live according to your values, you feel more authentic and confident because you're being true to yourself rather than trying to be someone you're not.

The exercises in this chapter will help you identify your natural abilities, discover what you truly care about, and learn how to use this self-knowledge to build lasting confidence.

EXERCISE 11

Strengths Scavenger Hunt

This exercise helps you identify your natural strengths by looking for evidence in your daily life and past experiences.

- ### *Instructions:*

Look through each category below and write down examples from your life that demonstrate these strengths. You might not have examples for every category, and that's okay—focus on the ones that feel true to you.

Communication Strengths:

- *Examples:* Good at explaining things, making people laugh, listening to friends, writing, public speaking, etc.

_____

_____

_____

_____

Creative Strengths:

- *Examples:* Artistic abilities, coming up with new ideas, problem-solving in unique ways, etc.

_____

_____

_____

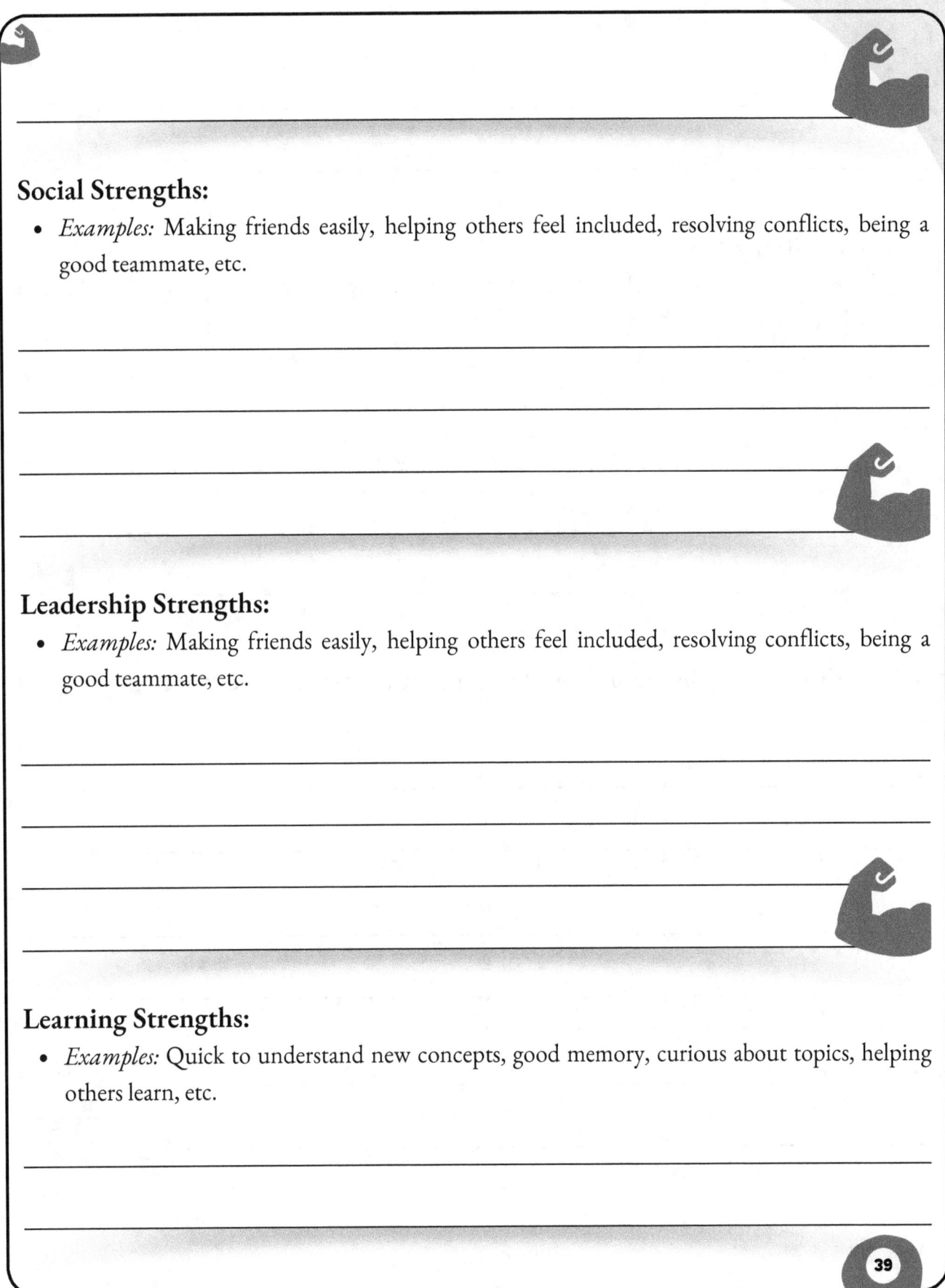

Social Strengths:

- *Examples:* Making friends easily, helping others feel included, resolving conflicts, being a good teammate, etc.

_____

_____

_____

_____

Leadership Strengths:

- *Examples:* Making friends easily, helping others feel included, resolving conflicts, being a good teammate, etc.

_____

_____

_____

_____

Learning Strengths:

- *Examples:* Quick to understand new concepts, good memory, curious about topics, helping others learn, etc.

_____

_____

_____

_____

_____

Character Strengths:

- *Examples:* Being honest, showing kindness, staying loyal to friends, persevering through challenges, etc.

_____

_____

_____

_____

Which three strengths from above feel most authentic to who you are?

1. _____

_____

2. _____

_____

3. _____

_____

EXERCISE 12

Values Compass

Your values act like a compass, guiding you toward decisions and actions that feel right. This exercise helps you identify what matters most to you.

• *Instructions:*

Look at the values listed below and circle the 10 that resonate most strongly with you. Then narrow it down to your top 5.

Adventure	Authenticity	Beauty	Belonging	Challenge	Community
Compassion	Creativity	Excellence	Fairness	Family	Freedom
Friendship	Fun	Growth	Health	Honesty	Independence
Justice	Knowledge	Leadership	Learning	Love	Loyalty
Nature	Peace	Recognition	Responsibility	Security	Service
Spirituality	Stability	Success	Tradition	Travel	Wisdom

My Top 10 Values *(circle above and list here)*:

- My Top 5 Values:

1. _____

2. _____

3. _____

4. _____

5. _____

- For each of your top 5 values, write one way you currently live this value:

1. _____

_____

2. _____

_____

3. _____

_____

4. _____

_____

5. _____

_____

EXERCISE 13

Past Success Stories

Looking at your past successes can reveal patterns about your strengths and help you remember times when you felt capable and confident.

- ### *Instructions:*

Think of five times in your life when you felt proud of something you accomplished. These can be big or small achievements.

Success Story 1:
- What happened:

_____

_____

_____

- What strengths did I use:

_____

_____

- How did I feel:

_____

_____

Success Story 2:

- What happened:

_____

_____

_____

- What strengths did I use:

_____

_____

- How did I feel:

_____

_____

Success Story 3:

- What happened:

_____

_____

_____

- What strengths did I use:

_____

_____

- How did I feel:

_____

_____

Success Story 4:
- What happened:

_____

_____

_____

- What strengths did I use:

_____

_____

- How did I feel:

_____

_____

Success Story 5:
- What happened:

_____

_____

_____

- What strengths did I use:

_____

_____

- How did I feel:

_____

_____

- What patterns do you notice in your success stories?

_____

_____

_____

_____

_____

EXERCISE 14

Skills That Come Naturally

Sometimes we take our natural abilities for granted because they feel easy to us. This exercise helps you recognize skills that might be strengths.

- ● *Instructions:*

Answer the following questions to identify abilities that come naturally to you.

- ● What do friends and family often ask for your help with?

_____

_____

_____

_____

- ● What activities make you lose track of time because you're so engaged?

_____

_____

_____

_____

- What compliments do you receive regularly?

_____

_____

_____

_____

- What seems hard for others but easy for you?

_____

_____

_____

_____

- What would you teach someone younger than you?

_____

_____

_____

_____

- When you were a child, what did adults say you were *"good at"* or *"natural at"*?

_____

_____

_____

_____

Based on your answers above, what are three natural skills you possess?

1. _____

_____

2. _____

_____

3. _____

_____

EXERCISE 15

Creating Your Personal Mission Statement

A personal mission statement combines your strengths and values to create a guide for how you want to live and what you want to contribute to the world.

- ### Instructions:

Use your discoveries from the previous exercises to create a personal mission statement.

- My key strengths are:

_____

_____

_____

- My core values are:

_____

_____

_____

- I want to use my strengths to:

_____

_____

_____

- I want to make a difference by:

- Complete this sentence: *"My mission is to..."*

- How does living according to this mission statement make you feel?

_____

_____

- What is one small action you can take this week to live more aligned with your mission?

_____

_____

_____

_____

Journal Prompts for Continued Growth

Take time to reflect on these questions in your own journal or notebook:

1.

How has discovering your strengths changed the way you see yourself?

2.

What would you do differently if you made decisions based on your values rather than what others expect?

3.

Which of your strengths do you want to develop further, and how could you do that?

4.

How can you use your unique combination of strengths and values to help others?

5.

What would you tell someone who says they *"aren't good at anything"*?

Chapter 4

Conquering Perfectionism

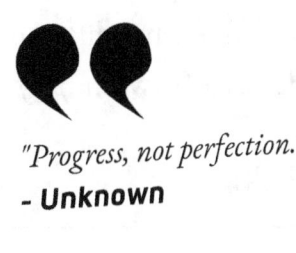

"Progress, not perfection."
- Unknown

Perfectionism might seem like a good thing—after all, don't we want to do our best? But perfectionism is different from having high standards. Perfectionism is the belief that anything less than perfect is a failure, and it often leads to procrastination, anxiety, and never feeling good enough.

CBT helps us understand that perfectionism is based on *"all-or-nothing thinking"*—a cognitive distortion where we see things as either completely successful or completely failed, with no middle ground. This type of thinking keeps us stuck because it makes us afraid to try new things, take risks, or show our work until it's *"perfect"* (which often means never).

The truth is, perfectionism doesn't lead to better results—it leads to paralysis, stress, and missed opportunities. Learning to embrace *"good enough"* and progress over perfection is essential for building genuine confidence and achieving your goals.

EXERCISE 16

The Good Enough Scale

This exercise helps you understand the difference between perfectionism and healthy standards by creating a scale of what *"good enough"* looks like in different areas of your life.

• *Instructions:*

For each area below, define what different levels of effort and outcome look like. This helps you see that there's a wide range between *"perfect"* and *"terrible."*

School/Homework:

Level	What this looks like
Perfectionist (100%)	
Excellent (90%)	
Good (80%)	
Acceptable (70%)	
Below Standard (60%)	
Unacceptable (50% or below)	

Social Situations:

Level	What this looks like
Perfectionist (100%)	
Excellent (90%)	
Good (80%)	
Acceptable (70%)	
Below Standard (60%)	
Unacceptable (50% or below)	

- Looking at your scales above, what percentage represents *"good enough"* for most situations?

_____

_____

_____

_____

- How does it feel to give yourself permission to aim for *"good enough"* instead of perfect?

_____

_____

_____

_____

_____

EXERCISE 17

Mistake Reframe Challenge

Perfectionism makes us fear mistakes, but mistakes are actually valuable learning opportunities. This exercise helps you reframe your relationship with making errors.

- ### *Instructions:*

Think of three recent mistakes you made and practice reframing them as learning experiences.

Mistake 1:
- What happened:

_____

_____

_____

- What I learned from it:

_____

_____

_____

- How it helped me grow:

_____

_____

_____

Mistake 2:

- What happened:

_____

_____

_____

- What I learned from it:

_____

_____

_____

- How it helped me grow:

_____

_____

_____

Mistake 3:

- What happened:

_____

_____

_____

- What I learned from it:

_____

_____

_____

- How it helped me grow:

_____

_____

_____

- **Complete this sentence:** _"Mistakes are valuable because..."_

_____

_____

_____

- What would you tell a friend who was beating themselves up over a mistake?

_____

_____

_____

_____

EXERCISE 18

Progress Over Perfection Journal

This exercise helps you shift your focus from perfect outcomes to meaningful progress and effort.

- ### *Instructions:*

For one week, instead of focusing on whether you did things perfectly, track your progress and effort in different areas.

Day	Activity/Task	Effort I Put In (1-10)	Progress I Made	What I'm Proud Of
Monday				
Tuesday				
Wednesday				
Thursday				
Friday				
Saturday				
Sunday				

- At the end of the week, what did you notice about focusing on progress instead of perfection?

_____

_____

_____

_____

_____

EXERCISE 19

The 80% Rule Practice

The 80% rule suggests that doing something at 80% effort often produces great results while saving time and reducing stress. This exercise helps you practice applying this principle.

- ### *Instructions:*

Choose three tasks or activities you need to do this week and practice the 80% rule with each one.

Task 1:

- What is it:

_____

_____

- What would 100% (perfectionist) effort look like:

_____

_____

_____

_____

- What will 80% effort look like:

_____

_____

_____

_____

- Results of using 80% effort:

_____

_____

_____

_____

Task 2:

- What is it:

_____

_____

- What would 100% (perfectionist) effort look like:

_____

_____

_____

_____

- What will 80% effort look like:

_____

_____

_____

_____

- Results of using 80% effort:

_____

_____

_____

_____

Task 3:
- What is it:

_____

_____

- What would 100% (perfectionist) effort look like:

_____

_____

_____

_____

- What will 80% effort look like:

_____

_____

_____

_____

- Results of using 80% effort:

_____

_____

_____

_____

- What surprised you about using the 80% rule?

_____

_____

_____

_____

_____

_____

EXERCISE 20

Failure as Feedback Activity

Perfectionism makes us avoid situations where we might fail, but failure often provides the most valuable feedback for improvement.

- ***Instructions:***

Think about an area where you've been avoiding taking action because you're afraid of not doing it perfectly.

- What have you been avoiding because you're afraid of failing?

_____

_____

_____

_____

- What's the worst realistic outcome if you try and don't do it perfectly?

_____

_____

_____

_____

- What's the best realistic outcome if you try?

_____

_____

_____

_____

- What feedback could you get from trying, even if it doesn't go perfectly?

_____

_____

_____

_____

_____

- What's one small step you could take toward trying this, even if you can't do it perfectly?

_____

_____

_____

Create a plan for taking this step:

- When will you do it:

_____

_____

- How will you prepare:

_____

_____

_____

- How will you celebrate trying, regardless of the outcome:

_____

_____

_____

After you try it, reflect on what happened:

- What went well:

_____

_____

_____

_____

- What you learned:

_____

_____

_____

_____

- What you'll do differently next time:

_____

_____

_____

_____

Journal Prompts for Continued Growth

Take time to reflect on these questions in your own journal or notebook:

1.
Where did you learn that you needed to be perfect? What messages did you receive growing up about making mistakes?

2.
How has perfectionism held you back from trying new things or taking risks?

3.
What would you attempt if you knew it was okay to not do it perfectly the first time?

4.
How do you feel about other people when they make mistakes? Are you more forgiving of others than yourself?

5.
What would change in your daily stress levels if you embraced *"good enough"* in more areas of your life?

Chapter 5

Building Body Confidence

"Your body is not your masterpiece —your life is."
- Glennon Doyle

Body image struggles are incredibly common during the teenage years. Your body is changing, you're comparing yourself to others, and you're bombarded with unrealistic images on social media and in the media. It's easy to get caught up in criticizing your appearance and forgetting about all the amazing things your body does for you every day.

CBT teaches us that our thoughts about our bodies directly impact how we feel and behave. When we have negative thoughts about our appearance, we might avoid social situations, stop participating in activities we enjoy, or spend hours worrying about how we look. But when we learn to appreciate our bodies for their function and treat them with respect, our confidence naturally improves.

Building body confidence isn't about thinking you're the most beautiful person in the world—it's about developing a healthy, respectful relationship with your body and recognizing that your worth as a person has nothing to do with your appearance.

EXERCISE 21

Body Appreciation Letter

This exercise helps you shift focus from what you don't like about your body to appreciating what it does for you.

- *Instructions:*

Write a letter to your body, thanking it for all the ways it serves you. Focus on function over form.

Dear Body,

Thank you for... *(Think about movement, healing, sensing the world, etc.)*

_____

_____

_____

_____

_____

_____

_____

_____

_____

I'm sorry for the times I... *(Think about criticism, harsh treatment, comparison, etc.)*

_____

_____

_____

_____

_____

_____

_____

I promise to treat you better by... *(Think about nourishment, rest, movement, kind thoughts, etc.)*

_____

_____

_____

_____

_____

_____

_____

I appreciate these specific things you do for me every day:

1. _____

_____

2. _____

_____

3. _____

_____

4. _____

_____

5. _____

_____

With respect and gratitude,

(_____)

Your name

EXERCISE 22

Function Over Form Focus

This exercise helps you recognize and celebrate what your body can do rather than only focusing on how it looks.

- ● *Instructions:*

Fill out the categories below, focusing on your body's capabilities and functions.

My body helps me express myself by:

_____

_____

_____

_____

My body allows me to experience pleasure through:

(Think about taste, touch, music, movement, etc.)

_____

_____

_____

_____

My body helps me connect with others by:

(Think about hugs, playing sports, dancing, etc.)

_____

_____

_____

_____

My body shows strength when:

_____

_____

_____

_____

My body demonstrates endurance when:

_____

_____

_____

_____

My body shows flexibility or adaptability when:

_____

_____

_____

_____

Something amazing my body has healed from:

_____

_____

_____

_____

A skill my body has learned:

_____

_____

_____

_____

How does focusing on function instead of appearance change how you feel about your body?

_____

_____

_____

_____

_____

EXERCISE 23

Media Detox Challenge

This exercise helps you become aware of how media influences your body image and create healthier media habits.

- **Instructions:**

Track your media consumption for three days, then implement changes to create a more body-positive media environment.

Day 1-3: Media Awareness

Type of Media	Time Spent	Messages About Bodies	How It Made Me Feel
Social Media			
TV/Movies			
Magazines			
Advertisements			
YouTube/TikTok			
Other			

- What patterns did you notice?

_____

_____

_____

_____

_____

Media Detox Actions I Will Take:

- Accounts I will unfollow because they make me feel bad about my body:

_____

_____

_____

- Body-positive accounts I will follow instead:

_____

_____

_____

- Times/situations when I will limit media consumption:

_____

_____

_____

_____

- Alternative activities I'll do instead of scrolling:

_____

_____

_____

_____

- After implementing these changes for one week, how do you feel?

_____

_____

_____

_____

_____

_____

EXERCISE 24

Compliment Shift Practice

This exercise helps you give and receive compliments that focus on character, achievements, and actions rather than just appearance.

• *Instructions:*

Practice shifting away from appearance-based compliments to more meaningful ones.

Appearance-Based to Character-Based Compliment Practice:

Instead of saying...	I can say...
"You look so pretty today"	
"I love your outfit"	
"You're so skinny/fit"	
"Your hair looks amazing"	
"You have great style"	
"You look so pretty today"	

Meaningful compliments I can give to others:

(Focus on kindness, talents, efforts, character, etc.)

1.
_____

_____

2.
_____

_____

3.
_____

_____

4.
_____

_____

5.
_____

_____

Meaningful compliments I can give to others:

(Focus on kindness, talents, efforts, character, etc.)

_____

_____

_____

_____

Non-appearance compliments I hope to receive:

_____

_____

_____

_____

_____

_____

How does shifting focus away from appearance in compliments feel?

_____

_____

_____

_____

_____

_____

EXERCISE 25

Mirror Work Makeover

This exercise helps you change your relationship with mirrors from critical to neutral or positive.

- ### *Instructions:*

Transform your mirror interactions from criticism sessions to opportunities for self-compassion and appreciation.

Current Mirror Experience:

- What I usually think when I look in the mirror:

_____

_____

_____

_____

_____

_____

- What I usually think when I look in the mirror:

_____

_____

_____

NEW MIRROR WORK PRACTICE:

- ### Week 1: Neutral Observations

Instead of judgments, practice neutral observations like *"I have brown eyes"* or *"My hair is curly today."* Daily practice notes:

_____

_____

_____

_____

_____

_____

_____

- ### Week 2: Function Appreciation

Notice and appreciate what different parts of your body do for you. Daily practice notes:

_____

_____

_____

_____

_____

_____

_____

_____

• Week 3: Positive Affirmations

Look in the mirror and say positive affirmations about your character, not just appearance.

• *My personal affirmations:*

1. _____

2. _____

3. _____

4. _____

5. _____

• Daily practice notes:

_____

_____

_____

_____

_____

_____

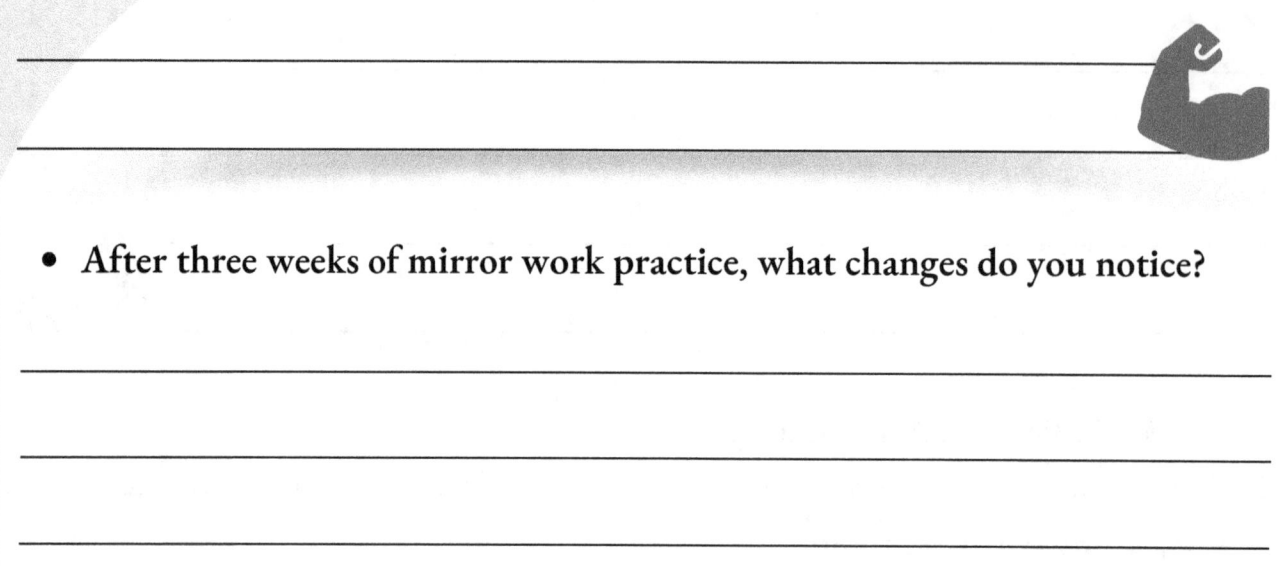

_____

_____

- **After three weeks of mirror work practice, what changes do you notice?**

_____

_____

_____

_____

_____

_____

Journal Prompts for Continued Growth

Take time to reflect on these questions in your own journal or notebook:

1.
What would you do differently if you weren't worried about how your body looked?

2.
How do you feel when you hear other people criticizing their own bodies? What would you want to tell them?

3.
What activities make you feel strong, capable, or connected to your body in a positive way?

4.
How has your relationship with your body changed as you've grown up? What do you miss about how you used to feel?

5.
What do you want to teach younger kids about body image and self-worth?

Chapter 6

Speaking Up and Setting Boundaries

"Daring to set boundaries is about having the courage to love ourselves, even when we risk disappointing others."

- Brené Brown

Many teens struggle with speaking up for themselves and setting healthy boundaries. You might worry about hurting others' feelings, being rejected, or coming across as mean or selfish. But learning to communicate your needs clearly and set appropriate boundaries is essential for building confidence and maintaining healthy relationships.

DBT teaches us interpersonal effectiveness skills—ways to get your needs met while maintaining your self-respect and your relationships with others. These skills help you ask for what you want, say no when you need to, and handle conflicts in a way that strengthens rather than damages your connections with people.

Setting boundaries isn't about being harsh or shutting people out—it's about creating clear guidelines for how you want to be treated and communicating those guidelines respectfully. When you can advocate for yourself effectively, you feel more confident and your relationships become healthier and more authentic.

EXERCISE 26

Boundary Setting Scripts

This exercise helps you develop clear, respectful language for setting boundaries in common situations teens face.

- ### *Instructions:*

For each scenario below, write a boundary-setting response using this formula: *"I feel _____ when _____ . I need _____ . Can you help me with that?"*

Scenario 1: Friend constantly borrows things without asking

- My boundary-setting response:

_____

_____

_____

_____

Scenario 2: Family member goes through your personal belongings

- My boundary-setting response:

_____

_____

_____

_____

Scenario 3: Friends pressuring you to do something you're uncomfortable with

- My boundary-setting response:

_____

_____

_____

_____

Scenario 4: Someone making jokes that hurt your feelings

- My boundary-setting response:

_____

_____

_____

_____

Scenario 5: Being asked to take on more responsibilities than you can handle

- My boundary-setting response:

_____

_____

_____

_____

Create your own challenging scenario and boundary response:

- Scenario:

_____

_____

_____

- My boundary-setting response:

_____

_____

_____

_____

Which of these scenarios feels most difficult for you to address? Why?

_____

_____

_____

_____

_____

_____

EXERCISE 27

The DEAR MAN Technique

DEAR MAN is a DBT skill for asking for what you want or saying no effectively. This exercise helps you practice using this structured approach.

- ### *Instructions:*

Learn the DEAR MAN formula, then apply it to a situation where you need to communicate something important.

DEAR MAN stands for:

- Describe the situation objectively
- Express how you feel
- Assert your needs clearly
- Reinforce the benefits of getting your needs met
- Mindful - stay focused on your goal
- Appear confident in your body language and tone
- Negotiate when possible

Practice Situation:

- What do you need to communicate?

_____

_____

_____

_____

Apply DEAR MAN:

Describe:

- What are the facts of the situation?

_____

_____

_____

_____

Express:

- How do you feel about it?

_____

_____

_____

Assert:

- What specifically do you want or need?

_____

_____

_____

_____

Reinforce:

- What are the positive outcomes if your needs are met?

_____

_____

_____

_____

Mindful:

- What's your main goal? How will you stay focused on it?

_____

_____

_____

Appear confident:

- How will you use confident body language and tone?

_____

_____

_____

Negotiate:

- What compromises might you be willing to make?

_____

_____

_____

Put it all together - write out what you would say:

EXERCISE 28

Saying No Practice

Learning to say no respectfully but firmly is crucial for maintaining boundaries and preventing burnout.

- ### *Instructions:*

Practice different ways to say no in various situations, from gentle to firm.

Gentle No (for small requests):
- *"I wish I could help, but I can't right now."*
- *"That sounds fun, but it's not for me."*

Your versions:

1. _____

_____

2. _____

_____

Clear No (for bigger requests):
- *"I've thought about it, and I won't be able to do that."*
- *"I'm not comfortable with that, so I'm going to pass."*

Your versions:

1. _____

_____

2. _____

_____

Firm No (for persistent pressure):

- _"I've already said no, and I need you to respect that."_
- _"I'm not changing my mind about this."_

Your versions:

1. _____

_____

2. _____

_____

Practice Scenarios:

Situation	Type of No Needed	What I Would Say
Friend asks to copy homework		
Invited to party you don't want to attend		
Asked to lie for someone		

Pressure to try something dangerous		
Extra responsibilities you can't handle		

- What makes saying no most difficult for you?

_____

_____

_____

_____

- How can you remind yourself that saying no is okay?

_____

_____

_____

_____

EXERCISE 29

Confidence Body Language

Your body language communicates as much as your words. This exercise helps you project confidence even when you don't feel it inside.

- **Instructions:**

Practice confident body language and notice how it affects how you feel and how others respond to you.

Confident Body Language Checklist:

Body Language Element	Confident Version	How I Usually Do This
Posture	Stand/sit up straight, shoulders back	
Eye Contact	Look people in the eyes when speaking	
Voice Volume	Speak loudly enough to be heard clearly	
Hand Gestures	Keep hands visible, use purposeful gestures	
Facial Expression	Relaxed, open expression	

Walking	Walk with purpose, steady pace	
Personal Space	Take up appropriate space, don't shrink	

Daily Practice Challenge:

- Choose one element of confident body language to focus on each day for a week.

Day 1 - Focus:

_____

- What I noticed:

_____

_____

_____

Day 2 - Focus:

_____

- What I noticed:

_____

_____

_____

Day 3 - Focus:

_____

- What I noticed:

_____

_____

_____

Day 4 - Focus:

_____

- What I noticed:

_____

_____

_____

Day 5 - Focus:

_____

- What I noticed:

_____

_____

_____

- How did practicing confident body language affect your interactions?

_____

_____

_____

_____

_____

Voice Volume Check

Many people, especially teens, speak too quietly when they're nervous or unsure. This exercise helps you find your confident speaking voice.

- ## *Instructions:*

Practice speaking at different volumes and in different situations to build vocal confidence.

Volume Practice Scale (1-10):

- 1-2: Whisper 3-4: Very quiet, hard to hear 5-6: Normal conversation volume 7-8: Confident, clear speaking 9-10: Loud, projecting voice

Practice Situations:

Ordering food at a restaurant:

- Current volume level:

_____

- Goal volume level:

_____

- Practice results:

_____

_____

_____

Answering questions in class:

- Current volume level:

_____

- Goal volume level:

_____

- Practice results:

_____

_____

_____

Talking to friends in a group:

- Current volume level:

_____

- Goal volume level:

_____

- Practice results:

_____

_____

_____

Speaking up when something bothers you:

- Current volume level:

_____

- Goal volume level:

_____

- Practice results:

_____

_____

_____

Vocal Confidence Tips I Want to Remember:

1. _____

_____

2. _____

_____

3. _____

_____

4. _____

- How does speaking with appropriate volume change how you feel about yourself?

_____

_____

_____

_____

_____

_____

Journal Prompts for Continued Growth

Take time to reflect on these questions in your own journal or notebook:

1.
What boundaries do you most need to set in your current relationships? What's been holding you back?

2.
How were boundaries modeled in your family growing up? What did you learn about speaking up for yourself?

3.
What's the difference between being assertive and being aggressive? How can you be firm while still being respectful?

4.
When you successfully advocate for yourself, how does it feel? How does it affect your confidence?

5.
What would you want to teach a younger sibling about standing up for themselves?

Chapter 7

Handling Setbacks and Building Resilience

"It's not about how hard you fall, it's about how you get back up."

- Vince Lombardi

Life will inevitably include setbacks, disappointments, and difficult times. The difference between people who thrive and those who get stuck isn't that thriving people don't face challenges—it's that they've learned how to bounce back from difficulties and use setbacks as opportunities to grow stronger.

Resilience is like a muscle that gets stronger with practice. DBT teaches us distress tolerance skills —ways to get through tough times without making them worse. These skills help you cope with intense emotions, ride out difficult situations, and recover more quickly from disappointments.

Building resilience doesn't mean pretending everything is fine when it's not, or trying to be positive all the time. It means developing the skills to handle life's ups and downs with grace, learning from setbacks, and maintaining hope even during difficult periods.

EXERCISE 31

The Resilience Timeline

This exercise helps you recognize that you've already overcome challenges in your life, which proves you have resilience within you.

- ### *Instructions:*

Create a timeline of challenges you've faced and overcome. Include both big and small difficulties.

Age/Time Period	Challenge I Faced	How I Got Through It	What I Learned

- Looking at your timeline, what patterns do you notice in how you handle challenges?

_____

_____

_____

_____

_____

- What strengths have you consistently used to get through difficult times?

_____

_____

_____

_____

_____

- How can this timeline remind you of your resilience during future setbacks?

_____

_____

_____

_____

_____

Setback Recovery Plan

This exercise helps you create a personalized plan for bouncing back when things don't go as expected.

- ***Instructions:***

Think about a recent setback or disappointment, then create a recovery plan using the steps below.

Recent setback or disappointment:

_____

_____

_____

_____

Step 1: Allow yourself to feel disappointed
- How will you give yourself permission to feel upset without judgment?

_____

_____

_____

_____

Step 2: Get perspective

- How big will this setback seem in 1 month? 1 year? 5 years?

_____

_____

_____

_____

_____

_____

Step 3: Learn from the experience

- What can this setback teach you? What would you do differently?

_____

_____

_____

_____

_____

_____

Step 4: Focus on what you can control

- What aspects of moving forward are within your control?

_____

_____

_____

_____

_____

_____

Step 5: Take action

- What's one small step you can take toward moving forward?

_____

_____

_____

_____

Step 6: Seek support

- Who can you talk to for encouragement or advice?

_____

_____

_____

_____

Create your personal setback recovery checklist:

- [ ] _____
- [ ] _____
- [ ] _____
- [ ] _____
- [ ] _____

EXERCISE 33

Emotional Regulation Toolkit

This exercise helps you build a collection of healthy coping strategies for managing intense emotions during difficult times.

- ### *Instructions:*

Create your personal toolkit of strategies for different types of emotional situations.

When I feel overwhelmed:

- Immediate relief strategies (0-5 minutes):

1. _____

_____

2. _____

_____

3. _____

_____

- Short-term coping strategies (5-30 minutes):

1. _____

_____

2. _____

_____

3. _____

_____

When I feel angry:

1. _____

_____

2. _____

_____

3. _____

_____

- Ways to cool down:

1. _____

_____

2. _____

_____

3. _____

_____

When I feel sad or hopeless:

- Comfort strategies:

1. _____

_____

2. _____

_____

3. _____

_____

- Mood-lifting activities:

1. _____

_____

2. _____

_____

3. _____

_____

When I feel anxious:

- Grounding techniques:

1. _____

_____

2. _____

_____

3. _____

_____

- Calming activities:

1. _____

_____

2. _____

_____

3. _____

_____

Emergency support contacts:

_____

_____

_____

_____

_____

_____

EXERCISE 34

Growth Mindset Mantras

This exercise helps you develop positive self-talk that supports resilience and growth during challenging times.

- ### Instructions:

Create personal mantras that help you maintain a growth mindset when facing difficulties.

Fixed Mindset vs. Growth Mindset Reframes:

Fixed Mindset Thought	Growth Mindset Reframe
"I'm terrible at this"	
"I'll never get better"	
"This is too hard"	
"I should give up"	
"Everyone else is better than me"	
"I can't handle this"	
"This always happens to me"	

My Personal Resilience Mantras:

(Create 5-10 short phrases you can repeat during tough times)

1. _____
   _____

2. _____
   _____

3. _____
   _____

4. _____
   _____

5. _____
   _____

6. _____
   _____

7. _____
   _____

Choose your top 3 mantras and practice saying them out loud:

Mantra 1:

_____

- How does it feel to say this?

_____

_____

_____

Mantra 2:

_____

_____

- How does it feel to say this?

_____

_____

_____

Mantra 3:

_____

_____

- How does it feel to say this?

_____

_____

_____

EXERCISE 35

The Phoenix Rising Activity

This exercise helps you identify how challenges have made you stronger and more capable, like a phoenix rising from ashes.

- ***Instructions:***

Think about a significant challenge you've overcome and explore how it contributed to your growth.

My Phoenix Story:

The Challenge (The Ashes):

- Describe a difficult time in your life:

_____

_____

_____

_____

_____

_____

_____

The Struggle (The Fire):

- What was the hardest part? What did you have to endure?

_____

_____

_____

_____

_____

_____

_____

The Transformation (Rising from the Ashes):

- How did you change or grow through this experience?

_____

_____

_____

_____

_____

_____

_____

New Strengths I Discovered:

1. _____

_____

2. _____

_____

3. _____

_____

4. _____

_____

Skills I Developed:

1. _____

_____

2. _____

_____

3. _____

_____

How I'm Different Now (The New Phoenix):

_____

_____

_____

_____

_____

_____

_____

What This Experience Taught Me About My Own Resilience:

_____

_____

_____

_____

_____

_____

_____

How can you use this phoenix story to encourage yourself during future challenges?

_____

_____

_____

_____

_____

_____

_____

Journal Prompts for Continued Growth

Take time to reflect on these questions in your own journal or notebook:

1.
What does resilience look like in your family or community? Who are your resilience role models?

2.
What's the difference between giving up and knowing when to change course? How do you tell the difference?

3.
How do you want to be remembered for the way you handle challenges and setbacks?

4.
What advice would you give to someone going through a difficult time similar to one you've experienced?

5.
How has facing challenges changed your perspective on what's truly important in life?

Chapter 8

Creating Supportive Relationships

"Surround yourself with people who believe in your dreams, encourage your ideas, support your ambitions, and bring out the best in you."

- Roy T. Bennett

The relationships in your life have a huge impact on your self-confidence. When you're surrounded by people who support, encourage, and accept you, it's much easier to feel good about yourself. But when you're around people who are critical, competitive, or unsupportive, it can drain your confidence and make you question your worth.

DBT teaches us that healthy relationships are built on mutual respect, clear communication, and appropriate boundaries. Learning to identify which relationships lift you up versus those that bring you down is crucial for protecting your mental health and maintaining your confidence.

Building supportive relationships isn't just about finding the right people—it's also about being a supportive person yourself and knowing how to nurture the connections that matter most to you.

EXERCISE 36

Relationship Audit

This exercise helps you evaluate the relationships in your life and identify which ones support your confidence and which ones might be holding you back.

- **Instructions:**

List the important people in your life and honestly assess how each relationship affects your self-esteem and well-being.

Person	How they make me feel about myself	How I feel after spending time with them	What they contribute to my life	Overall impact (+ or -)

Relationships that lift me up:

_____

_____

_____

_____

_____

_____

Relationships that drain my energy or confidence:

_____

_____

_____

_____

_____

_____

What patterns do you notice in your most supportive relationships?

_____

_____

_____

_____

_____

What changes do you want to make based on this audit?

_____

_____

_____

_____

_____

_____

EXERCISE 37

Support Network Map

This exercise helps you identify and strengthen your support network by mapping out different types of support you need and who provides them.

- ### *Instructions:*

Create a visual map of your support network by identifying who you can turn to for different types of support.

Types of Support:

- Emotional Support (people who listen and care):

1. _____

_____

2. _____

_____

3. _____

_____

- Practical Support (people who help with tasks/problems):

1. _____

_____

2. _____

_____

3. _____

_____

- Fun/Social Support (people you enjoy spending time with):

1. _____

_____

2. _____

_____

3. _____

_____

- Advice/Guidance Support (people you trust for wisdom):

1. _____

_____

2. _____

_____

3. _____

_____

- Encouragement Support (people who believe in you):

1. _____

_____

2. _____

_____

3. _____

_____

Gaps in my support network:

- What type of support do you need more of?

_____

_____

_____

_____

_____

_____

- How can you strengthen existing supportive relationships?

_____

_____

_____

_____

_____

_____

_____

• How can you find new supportive connections?

_____

_____

_____

_____

_____

_____

EXERCISE 38

Toxic Relationship Red Flags

This exercise helps you identify warning signs of unhealthy relationships that can damage your self-esteem.

• *Instructions:*

Learn to recognize red flags in relationships and reflect on any patterns you've experienced.

Relationship Red Flags Checklist:

- Check any that you've experienced in current or past relationships:

  ☐ Makes fun of you in front of others
  ☐ Constantly criticizes you or puts you down
  ☐ Tries to control what you do, wear, or who you spend time with
  ☐ Gets angry when you succeed or feel good about yourself
  ☐ Pressures you to do things you're not comfortable with
  ☐ Makes you feel like you have to *"earn"* their friendship/love
  ☐ Talks about you behind your back
  ☐ Is only nice to you when they want something
  ☐ Makes everything about them
  ☐ Gets jealous of your other relationships
  ☐ Threatens to end the relationship to manipulate you
  ☐ Makes you feel like you're *"walking on eggshells"*
  ☐ Dismisses your feelings or tells you you're *"too sensitive"*
  ☐ Competes with you instead of supporting you

Reflecting on red flags:

- Which red flags have you experienced?

_____

_____

_____

_____

_____

_____

- How did these behaviors affect your self-confidence?

_____

_____

_____

_____

_____

- What would you tell a friend who was experiencing these red flags?

_____

_____

_____

_____

_____

_____

_____

_____

Healthy relationship signs I want to look for:

1. _____

_____

2. _____

_____

3. _____

_____

4. _____

_____

5. _____

_____

If you're currently in a relationship with red flags, what support do you need to address this?

_____

_____

_____

_____

_____

_____

_____

EXERCISE 39

Building New Friendships Guide

This exercise provides a practical approach to forming new, healthy friendships based on shared interests and values.

- ● *Instructions:*

Create a plan for meeting new people and building friendships that support your confidence and well-being.

What I'm looking for in new friendships:

- ● Values that are important to me in friends:

1. _____

_____

2. _____

_____

3. _____

_____

4. _____

_____

- Activities/interests I'd like to share with friends:

1. _____

_____

2. _____

_____

3. _____

_____

4. _____

_____

- Qualities I bring to friendships:

1. _____

_____

2. _____

_____

3. _____

_____

4. _____

_____

Places/activities where I might meet like-minded people:

- At school:

_____

_____

_____

_____

- In my community:

_____

_____

_____

_____

- Through hobbies/interests:

_____

_____

_____

_____

- Online communities (safe ones):

_____

_____

_____

_____

Friendship-building action plan:

- This week I will:

_____

_____

_____

_____

- This month I will:

_____

_____

_____

_____

Conversation starters I can use:

1. _____

_____

2. _____

_____

3. _____

_____

EXERCISE 40

Self-Advocacy Practice

This exercise helps you practice advocating for yourself in relationships while maintaining connection and respect.

- ### *Instructions:*

Practice different scenarios where you need to advocate for yourself in relationships.

Scenario 1: Friend consistently cancels plans last minute

- How this affects me:

_____

_____

_____

- What I want to communicate:

_____

_____

_____

_____

- How I'll approach this conversation:

_____

_____

_____

_____

_____

Scenario 2: Someone in my friend group makes comments that hurt my feelings

- How this affects me:

_____

_____

_____

- What I want to communicate:

_____

_____

_____

- How I'll approach this conversation:

_____

_____

_____

_____

_____

_____

Scenario 3: Family member doesn't respect my boundaries

- How this affects me:

_____

_____

_____

- What I want to communicate:

_____

_____

_____

- How I'll approach this conversation:

_____

_____

_____

_____

Your own scenario:

- Situation I need to address:

_____

_____

_____

- How this affects me:

_____

_____

- What I want to communicate:

_____

_____

_____

_____

- How I'll approach this conversation:

_____

_____

_____

_____

_____

Self-advocacy reminders:

- You deserve to be treated with respect
- It's okay to have needs and express them
- Healthy relationships can handle honest communication
- You can be kind and firm at the same time

Journal Prompts for Continued Growth

Take time to reflect on these questions in your own journal or notebook:

1.

How do your closest relationships reflect your values and support your goals?

2.

What patterns do you notice in the relationships that have hurt your confidence? How can you avoid these patterns in the future?

3.

How do you want to show up as a friend to others? What kind of friend do you want to be remembered as?

4.

What would change in your life if you surrounded yourself only with people who genuinely support and encourage you?

5.

How can you better support the people in your life who lift you up?

Daily Habits for Lasting Confidence

Chapter 9

"We are what we repeatedly do. Excellence, then, is not an act, but a habit."
- Aristotle

Building lasting confidence isn't about one big breakthrough moment—it's about the small, consistent actions you take every day. Your daily habits shape your thoughts, emotions, and behaviors over time, which means they have a powerful impact on your overall self-esteem and well-being.

The habits that build confidence are often simple, but they require consistency to be effective. When you regularly engage in activities that support your mental health, honor your values, and reinforce positive self-talk, these practices become automatic parts of your life that continuously strengthen your inner foundation.

This chapter focuses on creating sustainable daily and weekly routines that naturally boost your confidence without feeling overwhelming or time-consuming. The goal is to integrate these practices so seamlessly into your life that they become as natural as brushing your teeth.

EXERCISE 41

Morning Confidence Ritual

This exercise helps you design a morning routine that sets a positive tone for your entire day and reinforces your commitment to treating yourself well.

- ### *Instructions:*

Create a personalized morning routine that includes elements that make you feel grounded, positive, and prepared for the day ahead.

Current morning routine:

- What do you usually do in the first hour after waking up?

_____

_____

_____

_____

_____

- How does your current routine make you feel?

_____

_____

_____

_____

Elements for a confidence-building morning routine:

- Choose 3-5 activities that appeal to you:

  ☐ Set daily intentions or goals
  ☐ Write down 3 things you're grateful for
  ☐ Say positive affirmations in the mirror
  ☐ Do 5-10 minutes of stretching or movement
  ☐ Listen to uplifting music
  ☐ Read something inspiring
  ☐ Practice deep breathing or meditation
  ☐ Write in a journal
  ☐ Review your personal strengths/values
  ☐ Plan something to look forward to
  ☐ Other:

_____

_____

My ideal morning routine:

- Time I want to wake up:

_____

- Activity 1 (5-10 minutes):

_____

_____

- Activity 2 (5-10 minutes):

_____

_____

- Activity 3 (5-10 minutes):

_____

_____

- Activity 4 (5-10 minutes):

_____

_____

- Activity 5 (5-10 minutes):

_____

_____

One-week trial:

- Track how your new morning routine affects your mood and confidence throughout the day.

Day	Which activities did you do?	How did you feel during the day?
Monday		
Tuesday		
Wednesday		
Thursday		
Friday		
Saturday		
Sunday		

- What did you notice about the connection between your morning routine and your daily confidence?

_____

_____

_____

_____

_____

_____

EXERCISE 42

Gratitude and Achievement Log

This exercise helps you develop the habit of regularly acknowledging both what you're grateful for and what you've accomplished, no matter how small.

- **Instructions:**

Create a simple daily practice of recording gratitude and achievements to train your brain to notice positive aspects of your life.

Weekly Gratitude and Achievement Log:

Day	3 Things I'm Grateful For	2 Things I Accomplished	1 Thing I Did Well
Monday			
Tuesday			
Wednesday			
Thursday			
Friday			
Saturday			
Sunday			

Gratitude categories to help you think of different things:

- Relationships (people who care about you)
- Experiences (fun moments, learning opportunities)
- Your body and health (what your body can do)
- Environment (nature, your home, community)
- Personal qualities (your character strengths)
- Opportunities (chances to grow, try new things)

Achievement categories (remember, small counts too):

- Academic (understanding a concept, completing homework)
- Social (having a good conversation, helping someone)
- Personal care (eating well, getting enough sleep)
- Creative (drawing, writing, making something)
- Physical (exercise, sports, walking)
- Character (showing kindness, being honest, standing up for someone)

After one week of logging, what patterns do you notice?

_____

_____

_____

_____

_____

_____

How has this practice affected your overall outlook?

_____

_____

_____

_____

_____

_____

EXERCISE 43

Weekly Self-Care Planning

This exercise helps you intentionally plan activities that support your physical, emotional, and mental well-being.

- ### *Instructions:*

Design a weekly self-care plan that ensures you're regularly engaging in activities that recharge and support you.

Self-Care Categories:

Physical Self-Care (body and health):

- Activities that make you feel:

_____

_____

_____

_____

Emotional Self-Care (feelings and mental health):

- Activities that make you feel:

_____

_____

_____

_____

Social Self-Care (relationships and connection):

- Activities that make you feel:

_____

_____

_____

_____

Creative Self-Care (expression and fun):

- Activities that make you feel:

_____

_____

_____

_____

Spiritual/Meaning Self-Care (purpose and values):

- Activities that make you feel:

_____

_____

_____

Weekly Self-Care Schedule:

Day	Physical	Emotional	Social	Creative	Spiritual / Meaning
Monday					
Tuesday					
Wednesday					
Thursday					
Friday					
Saturday					
Sunday					

Emergency self-care list (for stressful days):

- Quick activities you can do when you need immediate support:

1. _____

_____

2. _____

_____

3. _____

_____

4. _____

_____

5. _____

_____

Positive Affirmation Creation

This exercise helps you develop personalized affirmations that feel authentic and meaningful to you, rather than using generic statements that don't resonate.

- ### *Instructions:*

Create affirmations based on your own values, strengths, and goals that you can use to reinforce positive self-talk.

Understanding effective affirmations:
- Use present tense (*"I am"* not *"I will be"*)
- Make them specific to you
- Focus on character and effort, not just outcomes
- Use words that feel genuine to you

Affirmations for different areas:

About my character:

- Based on your values and strengths from Chapter 3:

1. _____

_____

2. _____

_____

3. _____

_____

About my effort and growth:

1. _____

_____

2. _____

_____

3. _____

_____

About my relationships:

1. _____

_____

2. _____

_____

3. _____

_____

About handling challenges:

1. _____

172

_____

2. _____

_____

3. _____

_____

About my potential:

1. _____

_____

2. _____

_____

3. _____

_____

My top 5 daily affirmations:

- Choose the affirmations that feel most meaningful and authentic to you:

1. _____

_____

2. _____

_____

3. _____

_____

4. _____

_____

5. _____

_____

Daily affirmation practice plan:

- When will you say your affirmations?

_____

_____

- Where will you say them?

_____

_____

- How will you remember to do this?

_____

_____

EXERCISE 45

Energy Audit

This exercise helps you identify which activities, people, and situations give you energy versus those that drain it, so you can make more intentional choices about how you spend your time.

- ### *Instructions:*

Track your energy levels throughout different activities and interactions to understand what supports your well-being and confidence.

Energy-giving vs. Energy-draining assessment:

Activity/Situation/ Person	Energy Level Before (1-10)	Energy Level After (1-10)	Energy Gain/Loss

Top 5 energy-giving activities/people/situations:

1. _____

_____

2. _____

_____

3. _____

_____

4. _____

_____

5. _____

_____

Top 5 energy-draining activities/people/situations:

1. _____

_____

2. _____

_____

3. _____

_____

4. _____

_____

5. _____

_____

Based on your energy audit, what changes do you want to make?

- I want to do MORE of:

_____

_____

_____

_____

_____

_____

- I want to do LESS of:

_____

_____

_____

_____

_____

_____

Strategies for managing energy-draining situations I can't avoid:

_____

_____

_____

_____

_____

_____

_____

Journal Prompts for Continued Growth

Take time to reflect on these questions in your own journal or notebook:

1.
Which daily habits have had the biggest positive impact on your confidence and well-being?

2.
What time of day do you feel most energized and confident? How can you protect and make the most of this time?

3.
How do you want to feel at the end of each day? What habits would help you achieve that feeling?

4.
What small changes in your routine could have a big impact on your overall happiness?

5.
How can you maintain these positive habits even when life gets busy or stressful?

Chapter 10

Your Personal Confidence Action Plan

"The future belongs to those who believe in the beauty of their dreams."

- Eleanor Roosevelt

Y ou've learned powerful tools for building inner strength and confidence throughout this workbook. Now it's time to put everything together into a personalized action plan that will help you maintain and continue growing your confidence over time.

Real change happens when you consistently apply what you've learned and adapt these tools to fit your unique life circumstances. This final chapter is about creating a sustainable plan that you can use long after you've finished this workbook—one that grows and evolves with you as you continue developing into the confident person you're meant to be.

Remember, building lasting confidence is not a destination but a journey. There will be setbacks and challenging days, but you now have the skills to handle them with grace and bounce back stronger than before.

EXERCISE 46

Confidence Goals Setting

This exercise helps you set specific, achievable goals for your confidence journey based on what you've learned about yourself through this workbook.

- ### *Instructions:*

Reflect on your progress and set clear goals for continued growth in different areas of your life.

Looking back at where you started:

- How would you have described your confidence level at the beginning of this workbook?

_____

_____

_____

_____

_____

_____

- What were your biggest confidence challenges when you started?

_____

_____

_____

_____

_____

_____

Current confidence assessment:

- How would you describe your confidence level now?

_____

_____

_____

_____

_____

- What positive changes have you noticed in yourself?

_____

_____

_____

_____

_____

_____

_____

- Which tools or exercises from this workbook have been most helpful?

_____

_____

_____

_____

_____

_____

_____

Goal setting for continued growth:

Area	Current Challenge	Specific Goal	How I'll Achieve It
Self-Talk			
Body Image			
Social Situations			

Standing Up for Myself			
Handling Setbacks			

My top 3 confidence goals for the next 6 months:

Goal 1:

_____

_____

- Why this matters to me:

_____

_____

_____

- How I'll measure progress:

_____

_____

_____

Goal 2:

_____

_____

- Why this matters to me:

_____

_____

_____

- How I'll measure progress:

_____

_____

_____

Goal 3:

_____

_____

- Why this matters to me:

_____

_____

_____

- How I'll measure progress:

_____

_____

_____

EXERCISE 47

Trigger Situation Prep

This exercise helps you prepare for situations that typically challenge your confidence, so you can handle them more effectively when they arise.

- ### *Instructions:*

Identify your most challenging situations and create specific action plans for handling them with confidence.

My confidence challenge situations:

- Situation 1:

_____

_____

_____

- Why this is challenging for me:

_____

_____

_____

- Negative thoughts that typically arise:

_____

_____

_____

_____

- Tools I can use from this workbook:

_____

_____

_____

_____

_____

My action plan:

- Before:

_____

_____

_____

_____

- During:

_____

_____

_____

_____

- After:

_____

_____

_____

_____

- Situation 2:

_____

_____

_____

- Why this is challenging for me:

_____

_____

_____

_____

- Negative thoughts that typically arise:

_____

_____

_____

_____

- Tools I can use from this workbook:

_____

_____

_____

_____

_____

My action plan:

- Before:

_____

_____

_____

_____

- During:

_____

_____

_____

_____

- After:

_____

_____

_____

_____

- Situation 3:

_____

_____

- Why this is challenging for me:

_____

_____

_____

_____

- Negative thoughts that typically arise:

_____

_____

_____

_____

- Tools I can use from this workbook:

_____

_____

_____

_____

_____

_____

My action plan:

- Before:

_____

_____

_____

_____

- During:

_____

_____

_____

_____

- After:

_____

_____

_____

EXERCISE 48

Support System Activation Plan

This exercise helps you create a clear plan for accessing support when you need it, including both professional help and personal support networks.

• *Instructions:*

Identify your support resources and create a plan for reaching out when you need help maintaining your confidence and mental health.

MY SUPPORT NETWORK:

Family members I can talk to:

- Name:

_____

_____

- Best for:

_____

_____

- Name:

_____

_____

- Best for:

_____

_____

Friends I trust:

- Name:

_____

_____

- Best for:

_____

_____

- Name:

_____

_____

- Best for:

_____

_____

Adults/mentors I trust:

- Name/Role:

_____

_____

- Best for:

_____

_____

- Name/Role:

_____

_____

- Best for:

_____

_____

PROFESSIONAL RESOURCES:

School counselor/social worker:

- Name:

_____

_____

- How to contact:

_____

_____

Therapist/counselor (if applicable):

- Name:

_____

- Contact info:

_____

_____

CRISIS RESOURCES:

- National Suicide Prevention Lifeline: 988
- Crisis Text Line: Text HOME to 741741
- Local crisis line:

_____

_____

When to reach out for support:

- I will reach out to friends/family when:

_____

_____

_____

_____

- I will reach out to professional support when:

_____

_____

_____

_____

- I will use crisis resources when:

_____

_____

_____

_____

HOW TO ASK FOR HELP:

What I can say to friends/family:

- *"I'm struggling with _____ and could use someone to talk to." "I'm working on my confidence and would appreciate your support with _____."*

_____

- My Version:

_____

_____

_____

_____

What I can say to professionals:

- *"I've been feeling _____ and think it would help to talk to someone." "I'm interested in working on my self-confidence and mental health."*

- My Version:

Monthly Self-Esteem Check-in

This exercise creates a system for regularly assessing your progress and adjusting your approach to building confidence.

- ## *Instructions:*

Design a monthly check-in process to track your growth and identify areas that need attention.

MONTHLY CHECK-IN QUESTIONS:

Overall confidence assessment:

- How would I rate my overall confidence this month? (1-10): _____

- What went well this month in terms of my confidence?

_____

_____

_____

_____

_____

- What situations challenged my confidence this month?

_____

_____

_____

_____

_____

_____

- Which tools from this workbook did I use most often?

_____

_____

_____

_____

- Which tools do I need to practice more?

_____

_____

_____

_____

Progress on my confidence goals:

Goal	Progress This Month	Next Steps

Daily habits assessment:

Habit	How Consistent Was I? (1-10)	How Did It Impact My Confidence?
Morning routine		
Gratitude practice		
Positive self-talk		
Boundary setting		
Self-care activities		

Relationship assessment:

- How are my relationships supporting my confidence right now?

_____

_____

_____

_____

_____

Areas for focus next month:

1.

_____

_____

2.

_____

_____

3.

_____

_____

Monthly check-in schedule:

- I will do this check-in on:

_____

_____

- Reminder system I'll use:

_____

_____

Letter to Future Self

This final exercise helps you capture your current insights and create a message of encouragement for yourself to read in the future.

- ### *Instructions:*

Write a letter to yourself to open in 6 months, reflecting on your journey and offering encouragement for continued growth.

Dear Future Me,

Today's date:

/	/

As I finish this workbook, here's what I want you to remember about our confidence journey:

- What I've learned about myself:

_____

_____

_____

_____

_____

_____

_____

- The biggest changes I've made:

_____

_____

_____

_____

_____

- Tools that have been most helpful:

_____

_____

_____

_____

_____

- Challenges I've overcome:

_____

_____

_____

_____

_____

- What I'm most proud of right now:

_____

_____

_____

_____

_____

- My hopes for you (future me) by the time you read this:

_____

_____

_____

_____

_____

_____

_____

_____

If you're struggling when you read this, remember:

- You've overcome challenges before and you can do it again
- It's okay to ask for help - that's a sign of strength, not weakness
- Small steps forward still count as progress
- You are worthy of love and respect, especially from yourself

Personal reminder:

_____

_____

_____

_____

Specific goals I hope you've achieved:

1. _____

_____

2. _____

3. _____

_____

_____

Questions for you to reflect on when you read this:

- How have you grown since writing this letter?
- Which goals have you achieved? What new ones have emerged?
- What are you most grateful for in your life right now?
- How can you continue building on the confidence you've developed?

A final message of encouragement:

_____

_____

_____

_____

_____

_____

_____

With love and belief in your continued growth,

(_____)

Your name

P.S.

_____

_____

_____

_____

Your Confidence Journey Continues

Completing this workbook is a significant accomplishment, but remember that building confidence is an ongoing process. You now have a toolkit of evidence-based strategies that you can return to whenever you need them.

Some final reminders as you continue your journey:

- **Progress isn't always linear** - you'll have good days and challenging days, and both are normal
- **Small, consistent actions** create bigger changes than dramatic gestures
- **Your worth isn't determined by your confidence level** - you are valuable regardless of how confident you feel
- **It's okay to revisit these exercises** whenever you need a refresher or want to deepen your practice
- **Professional support** is always an option if you want additional guidance

You have everything within you to build the confident, authentic life you deserve. Trust the process, be patient with yourself, and remember that every step forward matters.

Conclusion

"Believe in yourself and all that you are. Know that there is something inside you that is greater than any obstacle."
- Christian D. Larson

Y ou've just completed a powerful journey of self-discovery and growth. By working through 50 exercises across 10 chapters, you've developed a comprehensive toolkit for building and maintaining inner strength throughout your life.

The path to lasting confidence isn't about reaching a destination where you never doubt yourself again. It's about developing the skills to navigate life's challenges with resilience, treat yourself with compassion, and recognize your inherent worth regardless of external circumstances.

Through this workbook, you've learned to:
- Recognize and challenge your inner critic
- Break free from the comparison trap that steals your joy
- Identify your unique strengths and values
- Overcome perfectionism and embrace *"good enough"*
- Build a positive relationship with your body
- Set healthy boundaries and communicate your needs
- Handle setbacks with grace and resilience
- Create supportive relationships that lift you up
- Establish daily habits that naturally boost your confidence
- Develop a personalized plan for continued growth

These aren't just temporary fixes—they're life skills that will serve you well into adulthood. The CBT and DBT techniques you've practiced are the same ones used by mental health professionals worldwide because they work. With consistent practice, they become as natural as any other skill you've mastered.

Remember that building confidence is like building physical strength—it requires regular practice to maintain and grow. There will be times when old patterns of self-doubt creep back in, and that's completely normal. When this happens, return to the exercises that were most helpful to you. This workbook is designed to be a resource you can use again and again throughout your life.

Your teenage years are a time of incredible growth and change. While this can feel overwhelming at times, it also means you have tremendous capacity to develop new ways of thinking and being. By investing in your confidence now, you're setting yourself up for a lifetime of greater happiness, stronger relationships, and more authentic self-expression.

You are worthy of love, respect, and all the good things life has to offer—not because of what you achieve or how you look, but simply because you exist. Your unique combination of strengths, experiences, and perspectives makes you valuable in ways that no one else can replicate.

As you move forward, carry with you the knowledge that you have the power to create positive change in your life. Every small step you take toward treating yourself with kindness and respect makes a difference. Every boundary you set, every negative thought you challenge, and every moment you choose self-compassion over self-criticism is an act of courage that builds your inner strength.

The world needs confident, authentic young people who know their worth and aren't afraid to shine their light. By doing the work to build your own confidence, you're not only improving your own life—you're also modeling for others what it looks like to treat yourself well and live authentically.

Keep growing, keep practicing,
and remember: you've got this.

About the Author

Richard Bass

Richard Bass is a well-established author with extensive knowledge and background on children's disabilities. He has also experienced first-hand many children and teens who deal with depression and anxiety. Richard also enjoys researching techniques and ideas to better serve students, as well as providing guidance to parents on how to understand and lead their children to success.

Richard wants to share his experience, research, and practices through his writing, as it has proven successful to many parents and students. He feels there is a need for parents and others around the child to fully understand the disability, or mental health of the child. He hopes that with his writing, people will be more understanding of children going through these issues.

In regards to his qualifications, Richard holds a bachelor's and master's degree in education as well as several certifications including Special Education K-12, and Educational Administration. Whenever he is not working, reading, or writing, he likes to travel with his family to learn about different cultures as well as get ideas from all around about the upbringing of children especially those with disabilities. He also researches and learns about different educational systems around the world.

Richard participates in several online groups where parents, educators, doctors, and psychologists share their successes with children with disabilities. He also has his own group where further discussion about his books and techniques take place. Apart from his participation in online groups, Richard also attends training related to the upbringing of students with disabilities and has also led training in this area.

When to Seek Additional Help

While this workbook provides valuable tools for building confidence, there are times when professional support is important:

Consider reaching out to a counselor, therapist, or trusted adult if you:

- Have thoughts of hurting yourself or others
- Feel hopeless or depressed for more than two weeks
- Are using substances to cope with difficult emotions
- Have experienced trauma that continues to affect your daily life
- Feel overwhelmed by anxiety despite using coping strategies
- Are engaging in behaviors that harm your health or relationships
- Feel like your emotions are out of control
- Have experienced significant changes in sleep, appetite, or energy levels

Crisis Resources:

- National Suicide Prevention Lifeline: 988
- Crisis Text Line: Text HOME to 741741
- National Teen Dating Abuse Helpline: 1-866-331-9474
- SAMHSA National Helpline: 1-800-662-4357

How to find ongoing support:

- Talk to your school counselor about resources in your area
- Ask your family doctor for referrals to teen-friendly therapists
- Look for community mental health centers that offer sliding scale fees
- Consider online therapy platforms that specialize in teen mental health (with parent permission)

Remember, asking for help is a sign of strength, not weakness. Professional counselors and therapists are trained to help you work through challenges that feel too big to handle alone.

Additional Resources for Continued Growth

Books:

- *"Mind Over Mood"* by Dennis Greenberger and Christine Padesky
- *"The Anxiety and Worry Workbook"* by David A. Clark and Aaron T. Beck
- *"The Self-Compassion Workbook"* by Kristin Neff
- *"Mindset"* by Carol Dweck

Apps:

- Headspace (meditation and mindfulness)
- Calm (relaxation and sleep)
- DBT Coach (DBT skills practice)
- Sanvello (mood and anxiety tracking)

Websites:

- Teen Mental Health: www.teenmentalhealth.org
- National Alliance on Mental Illness (NAMI): www.nami.org
- Centre for Addiction and Mental Health: www.camh.ca

Professional Resources:

- Psychology Today Therapist Directory: www.psychologytoday.com
- American Psychological Association: www.apa.org
- National Association of Social Workers: www.socialworkers.org

References

- Beck, A. T., Rush, A. J., Shaw, B. F., & Emery, G. (1979). Cognitive therapy of depression. Guilford Press.
- Beck, J. S. (2021). Cognitive behavior therapy: Basics and beyond (3rd ed.). Guilford Press.
- Harter, S. (1990). Causes, correlates, and the functional role of global self-worth: A life-span perspective. In R. J. Sternberg & J. Kolligian Jr. (Eds.), Competence considered (pp. 67-97). Yale University Press.
- Harter, S. (1999). The construction of the self: A developmental perspective. Guilford Press.
- Hirsch, B. J., & DuBois, D. L. (1991). Self-esteem in early adolescence: The identification and prediction of contrasting longitudinal trajectories. Journal of Youth and Adolescence, 20(1), 53-72.
- Keane, L., & Loades, M. E. (2017). Low self-esteem and internalizing disorders in young people: A systematic review. Child and Adolescent Mental Health, 22(1), 4-15.
- Linehan, M. M. (1991). Cognitive-behavioral treatment of chronically parasuicidal borderline patients. Archives of General Psychiatry, 48(12), 1060-1064.
- Linehan, M. M. (2014). DBT skills training manual (2nd ed.). Guilford Press.
- Linehan, M. M. (2015). DBT skills training handouts and worksheets (2nd ed.). Guilford Press.
- Linehan, M. M., & Wilks, C. R. (2015). The course and evolution of dialectical behavior therapy. American Journal of Psychotherapy, 69(2), 97-110.
- Mental Health Foundation. (2018). Stress: Are we coping? 2018 stress survey. Mental Health Foundation.
- Orth, U., & Robins, R. W. (2014). The development of self-esteem. Current Directions in Psychological Science, 23(5), 381-387.
- ROX Institute. (2023). The state of girls' mental health and self-confidence study. https://www.theroxinstitute.org/research

- Trzesniewski, K. H., Donnellan, M. B., Moffitt, T. E., Robins, R. W., Poulton, R., & Caspi, A. (2006). Low self-esteem during adolescence predicts poor health, criminal behavior, and limited economic prospects during adulthood. Developmental Psychology, 42(2), 381-390.
- World Health Organization. (2021). Adolescent mental health. https://www.who.int/news-room/fact-sheets/detail/adolescent-mental-health

www.ingramcontent.com/pod-product-compliance
Lightning Source LLC
Chambersburg PA
CBHW081656120626
46550CB00010B/2920